David Patterson Hatch

Some Philosophy of the Hermetics

David Patterson Hatch

Some Philosophy of the Hermetics

ISBN/EAN: 9783337070502

Printed in Europe, USA, Canada, Australia, Japan

Cover: Foto ©Thomas Meinert / pixelio.de

More available books at **www.hansebooks.com**

SOME PHILOSOPHY

OF THE

HERMETICS

ISSUED BY AUTHORITY OF THE

*There are some who will see and seeing will perceive,
others hearing will understand.*

1898
B. R. BAUMGARDT & CO.
PRINTERS AND PUBLISHERS,
LOS ANGELES, CAL.

CONTENTS.

TRADE

MARK

PREFACE.

Nature has a way of concealing and revealing. She tells half her story out in the sunshine in a loud voice, and the other half in whispers underground.

She is coy like a coquette, and stern like a judge. She excites curiosity in the student, and dread in the debauchee.

She holds the man of science to her breast, but is dumb to the lover of pleasure. She scorns the victim of priestcraft and repudiates the supernatural. The Sage takes his cue from his mother; like Nature, he conceals and reveals. He who would see other than the smiling, scowling *face* of Hermes must search the dark places by the light of his own candle; Hermes locks the gate between the outer and inner

Temple; and he, only, enters the latter, who has the pass word and the key.

In reading this book please notice how the essays vary in style; some of them falling into a weird rhapsody, others laconic and plain —The Mystic will understand the reason of the difference, while another will peruse only the words.

The barbaric splendor of Nature reveals truth and law as surely as does her terrible logic. She speaks in poetry and in prose. Facts are rarely ever naked, but often not only draped but masked. The occult eye sees straight to the heart of a fact, while the normal lens dwells on the habiliments.

Enough has been said save this — *Man inevitably cometh unto his own.*

THE HERMETICS.

Who were they? What are they? They were those who could speak or *keep silent.* They are those who whisper or shout. They believe in *silver* and *gold.* "If speech is silver silence is gold." They believe in the conservation of energy, and its transformation. They believe in the Unit and in the many—the special and the general. They have found the Philosopher's stone—the elixir of life. They catch glimpses of Eldorado—the promised land. They know time and realize eternity. They comprehend distance and space. They circumscribe the square with the circle, and death with life. They teach an eternity of being, and an endless variety of form. They wed involution to evolution, and yesterday to tomorrow. They insist on object as the mirror of subject, and consciousness as the child of the two. They hold that Nirvana is poise —a motionless motion—the paradox of being.

To find the Hermetic out of Thibet is to discover him next door. He is as likely to be in broadcloth as in adept's robe—and as possible in London as in Benares. He is rare. Gold is not picked up without stooping, nor the *fountain* head discovered without searching. Swine are about and pearls are treasured.

Enough, save this—The false implies the true.—Chaos, order.—The word, secrecy.— " *The one thing, many.*"

PHILOSOPHY.

With your heart filled with emotions, your head stormy with thought; with your back on the years behind you, facing the years ahead—*you*, a man, stand trembling with the consciousness of self, and wonder what next.

Philosophy ! ah me ! Philosophy !   When the heart beats to the tune of love, or your brain throbs with a master-passion—Philosophy ! you plunge headlong into life as the comet into space--living--living--living--only living.

Philosophy ! What need have you ? Your blood surges up to your heart and on to your head—you feel, you think—Philosophy ! Life is for life, you say—Philosophy ! but--but--you hav'nt it--life, only a shiver of it--only a thrill of it.

Philosophy brings it–life. She is beautiful—she carries a cup in her hand—it is gold; she begs you to drink and *live*. She is your hand-maiden—Philosophy—the cup is pure metal—the drink is elixir—*life*. As man, you are *mortal;* you have stood in the sunshine so long you are blind. As man, you are drunk with a *drop* of pure life; you have listened so long to the seas, you are deaf. Philosophy brings you the cup and you drink, and you open your eyes; she waits —and you listen and hear—what—what do you see—do you hear?

Yourself—in the sun, in the sea—yourself in the sky, in the air—yourself in the winds, in the stars—yourself in the depths, in the heights—yourself in the distance— yourself nearer home—yourself in the open —yourself in the closed—yourself in the seen and unseen—*yourself everywhere;* yourself in her eyes—Philosophy's eyes— yourself in her voice—Philosophy's voice— yourself in the speech of the beasts, in the song of the birds, the rustling of leaves; in nothing, in something, in naught and in all;

in negative, positive, neither and both; in
you and in other, in other and you.

Life!—inward and outward, receding ad-
vancing, coming and going—*Life!* Feeling
is feeling—thinking is thinking—*Life!*
Sleeping is sleeping—waking is waking—
Life! Living is living—dying is dying—
Life!

Open the windows and breathe the fresh
air—open the windows and look at the sky
—open the windows and feel the soft rain—
breathe—breathe—breathe full to the chest
—breathe.

I've traveled the spaces by thinking—I've
mounted the zenith by wishing—I've floated
in air by a longing—I've melted in mist
when a dreaming—I have flashed in the fire
by desiring—I have blended in water by
looking—I have entered a soul by aspiring.
I am many or one—I am one or the many.

Each day is mine own not anothers; each
day is all days, all days are each day.

I floated in blood in the veins of a bird,
and beat in his heart to the tune of his wings;
I sucked at the breast of a flower and dripped

in the honey of bees; I spun the fine silk of a web, and tied up the knots of a snare; I have lain in the arms of a cloud and turned up my face to the sky; I died and entered the tomb, and rotted away in a corpse; I crawled through the pores of the earth in the succulent bodies of worms, and buried myself in the mire to shiver with cold in a stone. Ah! Life and Philosophy! Wisdom and Life!

Do you ask me the reason of all, I give you the reason of none; do you ask me the reason of none, I give you the *wisdom* of all.

You burn with *desire* and you *thrill;* then dip in the blood of yourself and write on the parchment a scroll, and read in the letters the words, and read in the words the command, and in the command the design, and in the design, the beginning and end; and living you read, and reading you live; and cease to be mortal, but soar as a god.

If ever the bush is on fire harken for language and hear; something is speaking—listen and listen—something is shining—the bush is on fire.

FAITH.

We will present the subject of faith in a secondary aspect, and show you how to make out of it a mighty lever towards accomplishing results. We advise you to be *alert,* and in a certain sense skeptical in all save the principle upon which you found your premise.

Take as a starting point yourself, for it is not necessary to travel far from home in order to find a subject on which to work. Believing in your existence, a priori, and resting upon the fundamental consciousness of the Ego, suppose you branch out into a series of unusual experiments as to what the possibilities of that Ego are.

Most people find certain dominant tendencies uppermost, and are entirely satisfied to develop and live by them, never striving to discover hidden mines within themselves along lines where they have not taken the trouble to penetrate.

If you see a leaf floating on the wave at sea, you have some reason to think that land is near. May it not be possible that some indication as small as a leaf, floats round on the sea of your being, and you have failed to draw any conclusion from it. The mariner discovers the bit of green, and makes for the shore; you discover the sign of unseen things and sail out into deeper waters.

The lesson we would teach is this, observe the *signs,* no matter how insignificant; let them create in you a sort of *conditional* faith; follow them up and see what you will discover.

The scientist is well used to this conditional faith; it is not absolute faith, but a suspension of judgment, an abandonment of prejudice, and a simple research based upon indications. When the miner strikes a sign of color, a certain faith is developed in him; it is conditional of course; it is based on

possibility, not on probability. It is quite a
different thing from a man's faith in gravi-
tation or repulsion.   It is what might be
called a blind faith ; and the only excuse for
its being is that in time, it will develop into
a certainty or fall through altogether, in
other words prove itself.

Suppose for instance, you find at some
one time, that you have seen clairvoyantly,
treat that as the leaf on the sea of your
being ; follow it up, and be not astonished
if you land on the shore of an *unknown*
country.   Your faith which was suf-
ficient to lead you to explore, has brought
you a *certainty* which translates itself into
an added power.

The reason that we insist on a conditional
faith such as the scientist has, is this ; if you
blindly follow signs, so swallowed up in
your belief that you are incapacitated to
reason, or to think, or to bear disappoint-
ment, you will become fanatical, and lose
your discrimination and power of judgment.

There is a faith that is prepared for
either success or failure ; it is a kind of half

belief in a thing, still strong enough to lead
one to honest, unbiased investigation about
it.   It is the proper faith for one who inves-
tigates spiritualistic, psychic and sleight-of-
hand phenomena ; a watchful, fair, consider-
ate **faith** which **weighs** the pros and cons in
an investigation, **and** allows no undue influ-
ence **to** be brought **to bear either** for or
against the result sought.

This is strictly the *scientific faith*, and
it is the first essential in the mind of the
student **of** Philosophy.   **It should be** laid
down as an axiom **by all** beginners in the
pursuit of knowledge, that **our** *desiring* or
not desiring a thing to be, cuts no figure in
the investigation.   Truth **does** not arrange
herself **to suit us,** but forces **us** to conform
to her.

If we enter the study **of** Philosophy with
certain fixed ideas of what we would like to
have, and of how we wish the Universe to be
conducted, we are pretty apt **to** abandon the
pursuit when we come to find out that Truth
does not cut her clothes after **a** pattern of
our own designing.   Truth **is** safe enough

and we can not improve upon her. It is our business to pursue her, and catch and hold some aspect of her if possible, otherwise we had better return to our delusions.

To find Truth we must use the scientific method, which is always founded upon a temporary faith; a premise assumed for the time being, as a test of the possibility of the solution of the problem. This is not the supreme faith which is founded upon the principle of being, and must be the rock upon which we build up any lasting structure. It is the shifting faith which can be abandoned, as we find the object upon which it is fixed useful or not; but we do insist that when you start out to explore yourself, and to discover the latent possibilities within you, that you do as Columbus did, who hoped to find a new Continent, which up to the day when the first sign of land appeared, was to him and the whole of Europe an image and a dream.

CONCENTRATION.

We urged you in the last talk to go on a
voyage of discovery in yourself, and see if
some waking potentiality was awaiting
development. In this paper we desire to
insist on the use of concentration to this effect.
You who think you know how to concentrate, will find on attempt at a *sustained*
effort how difficult it is, and how weak you
are.

Look back and see how many things you
have begun, how many good resolutions you
have made, and how much you have
attempted and failed to complete.

Youth climbs up the ladder of his own
hopes and scans the prospect; he expects
to do every thing, to conquer every thing;
he levels mountains of opposition in his
own mind. He figures on becoming king

of opportunity and creating it at his own
bidding. Notice him ten years later sitting
at the foot of the ladder of his dreams. He
has spent his summers and his winters, his
springs and his autumns in *dabbling*.

First an attempt at this and then at
that, tasting here and there of everything
and nourished by nothing. He starts
down a road to view an object, and
slips off into a byway to view something
else. He gets to singing a new tune and
forgets the first stanza of the old one. He
knows people and forgets their names, or he
knows their names and forgets their faces.
He is forever experimenting and never
finishing; he rests half way up the mountain and a positive climax is something that
he knows nothing about.

Look over *your* life and see what you
have done. You have dipped into books,
but they never dipped into you. You have
studied human nature and been cheated a
hundred times. You have kissed a friend,
and then another without reading the heart
of the first. You came to the realm of

Philosophy, and wandered around in a maze;
you plucked a leaf and threw it away; you
inhaled the perfume of a flower and passed
on; you gathered a bouquet and tossed it
into the stream; you dabbled your feet in
the water, and washed your face in the dew;
and then, you entered the front door of a
church and passed out at the rear.

You tickled the wings of cupid, and he
flew away, and sitting down on a grave you
sighed; and the next week, you danced.
Such your life. Now you come to our doors
and knock; and we say to you, from behind
the lock, "Can you look at the point
of a pin—and *look* and *look*. Can you
rest on a premise, and think and think
up to the conclusion—can you pile up
facts on facts to the pinnacle of a principle—
can you study on one line to the very end of
the question—can you *act* on your conclusion as against the world—can you resist
straying to the right and left when you have
started towards a place or condition—can
you keep on aiming with the same stone at
the same spot till you *hit* it—can you stay

fixed in any pursuit any length of time, or are you a child?"

Start out with yourself and follow the leaf on the wave of your sea; follow—follow—concentrate and follow, by the blind faith of science, some sign in yourself till its value be disclosed. Be like the dog that gives chase, and is bound to be in at the death or the capture.

We tell you now, at the very inception of the study of Philosophy, that you must have two kinds of faith; one absolute, the other secondary and changeable; also *concentration;* without these it is useless to go on.

To cultivate concentration you must practice. Cultivate that bull-dog tenacity to hold on to a thing till you know what it is, if you have once decided to grapple with it.

Look into yourself and see if your past indicates concentration; if not, *begin.*

PRACTICE.

There is something **truly pathetic in the lives of** those who preach and do not practice; **who revel in** the generalities of Philosophy **as a sort of** intellectual tonic, and **are at** the same time too lazy to try the formulas and hold fast **to that** which **is good.**

I desire **you to avoid a** method **of practice that is** backed **by habit. To take** stated times to become good (say Sundays), **is not at all** after the manner of our system; **and if you** continually pursue this means, you will grow as fixed **as a rock** crystal.

Life **is your business, all** *kinds* **of life; rustling among** men, eating—drinking— **sleeping—just** as Christ did; **and the best time for you to practice, is** *all* **the time.**

I who give **you these instructions, know what life is from its** pleasures to its agonies;

from its feasts to its graveyards; and the more of a Philosopher I am, the more do I know of its fulness. So when I tell you to practice, I mean that you are to stay where *you are and practice.*

The great need of the world is the *living* Philosopher. Cloisters are out of date. Monasteries are old fashioned; they belong to the middle ages.

People must clash with each other in order to live; must feel each other's pulse, and jostle shoulder to shoulder; they must mingle magnetism, I might say, and give and take. In this rush, this hurry, is the time to try your cult and test its value.

If you hide a diamond in a box, it loses all its power to be saucy and throw back the sun's rays to the sun; in fact it forgets after a while that it is a diamond at all, and becomes as sullen as a cold pebble. If you have anything good, you must find it out; and you never can do that by shutting yourself up in an *occult* room and imagining.

Do not mistake us; we told you to concentrate, and contemplate the point of a pin,

but not *forever*. While a certain amount
of daily retirement into "your closet" is
good, just as rest is necessary after exercise,
too *much* of it is bad. Learn to concentrate
and act too; this is practice of the best kind.
Have a purpose, a means, a way, and ACT
on it. Having a theory and getting *no* fact
out of it, is like having a friend who will
never embrace you.

Concentration and action should go together. To be sure, you should reverse and
retire into yourself when the *occasion* de-
mands, but never *periodically* and to order.
Learn to do it when you have need of it (and
you can tell that) but do not do it because
you have arranged to.

We preach practice from morning until
night; all the time, everywhere. Your
Philosophy should stick to you closer than
the hairs of your head, and should put in an
appearance on every occasion. If it is good
for great things, it is good for little things.

This does not mean that you are to be like
the self-conscious christian who can never
get rid of his sense of responsibility; on the

contrary, it assures you the best that there is in life. It shows you how to extract the most honey from the flower, the grestest beauty from the landscape, and the truest love out of a fellow mortal. It is also a sort of accident policy, it bestows on you a weekly allowance in case of something unfortunate and unforeseen; and if you die, it pays up to the last penny those whom you have left behind.

It is practical, practical, practical, and if what you are getting is not, you hav'nt the right thing. Practice at all times, and whenever you fail in making the application, you are that far short of grasping the situation.

MEMORY.

When you go **down into the shadowy** place where the sun's rays **can not come, you** are reconciled **to** the gloom because you *remember*. What is it that you remember? That the sun **still** shines. You **know very well** that not a ray can penetrate where you are; **that as far** as **you are** concerned, for the time being, **the Giver** of Life—the Consoler—**the Sun—might as well be** put out. It **is a dark** place—gloom—gloom—gloom **every where, and along** with **the** gloom, dampness **and chill.** But **what of it—your** memory serves **you** well—you **recall the** splendor outside—the half hour ago **when** you basked **in heat** and color—all the tints that **the sun** brings out—all the brilliancy —and instead **of** a realization, **you** *substitute a **memory**.*

In your pursuit of Philosophy, understand that your path will *not* be all sunshine. Philosophy does not undertake to supply glory and glitter, nor does it guarantee you a freedom from shadows and tears. Philosophy does not undertake to change nature; it gives you no seven-leagued boots with which to stride over the land—no sandals like those of Pallas Athene, nor wings of a Mercury. Philosophy lets Dame Nature alone so far as changing her is concerned ; in fact she is very self-willed and like all feminine things, has her own way ; but here is a secret—Philosophy deals with nature somewhat as a good husband does with a stubborn spouse; Philosophy manages nature through her own attributes. A natural attribute by the way, is memory. Philosophy knowing this, brings it to bear at the right time, and reaps the reward. Philosophy has much tact, just as a wise husband has.

To use *art* in *remembering*, is an essential towards Philosophic life. To be a good forgetter, is as necessary as to be a good

recaller. There is nothing more uncomfortable and out of place, than to have something that you have **put** under the sod, protrude its head at the wrong time. When you bury, bury deep, and do not dig up the thing unless you want it.

Some memories are bores, just like some people ; they stay and stay **out of** pure viciousness, and the more you **curse** them **the** more staying power they **show.** **A** Philosopher will never allow this ; he knows that he **can** get rid of one memory by substituting another, just as you would shove **an** impertinent person out of **a** chair and put another in his place. As you can *forget* by a sort of *substitution,* you can *remember* by a *mental suggestion.*

When down **in the** shadow, recall something—a star, a diamond, **or a** friend's eyes; **and see how** quickly **the** place will **glow as if a** sun had **been** born, **with** dropped lids—it is the same. There **is a flash** and a shimmer in the fire of memory **which** radiates **in the** now, if you desire **it.**

Let us carry this lesson farther. Physical darkness is but *one* phase; there is a mental and a spiritual blackness which tongue can not speak of, nor pen portray. Even in this dungeon of dungeons memory can send a straight ray, and turn black to white, night to day. When you recall the sun, at the time shadows enshroud you, with that recollection comes the consciousness that the sun is a fixed fact—that it exists, and that *shadows* can not extinguish it; this makes you safe; safe in your mind, safe in your heart; you wrap the mantle of darkness about you, and laugh in the face of the night—for the sun IS. *You have remembered.*

When any trouble—gloom—mood, enfolds you in a cloud, remember that the *sun is*, and the rays are warm, *love* warm, and they shine somewhere *even* in your recollection, and with the remembering will come a flash like that of Jupiter on Olympus—like that of a friend's eyes— and black will turn to white and night to day.

This is the office of memory. Memory is your servant, if you can only realize it, memory is your slave, and all slaves impose upon their masters when allowed.

Put impertinent memories to sleep; wake up the right one at the right time; and cheat Dame Nature into believing that she has conquered Philosophy.

IMAGINATION.

To imagine something is to call up an image in the mind by the will. This is voluntary imagination. Involuntary imagination (which is a bad thing always) is that state where the image or images come of their own accord, oftentimes as unwelcome, vulgar or wicked guests.

Most lewd, vile, uncanny people are tools of the imagination. Images which seem to be like conscious entities, persist in dwelling in, and dominating the untrained tenant of an abused brain, and do incalculable mischief to him and those with whom he associates.

Imagination is man's greatest friend and his greatest enemy; if you control him he will serve you; and no artist can paint pictures as beautiful as his. Command him to

sketch the sea, the sky, the stars, the unseen
and seen wonders of earth and heaven, and
he will produce instantaneous results. He
will decorate your castle for you and place
you in it; he will create an interior environment that will so overpower your soul that
crude outer surroundings will cease to
trouble you.

Imagination controlled by the will, is the
one thing to be desired. On the other hand,
involuntary imagination, that creature which
like a snake slips into your sanctuary in the
dark and conceals itself to coil and sting
when you are totally unable to combat it, is
to be abhorred and dreaded. Not that he is
forever ugly—the serpent has an unrivaled
grace, and is a marvel in color—not that,
but he is unreliable, treacherous and poisonous; he may not sting, but if he does the
antidote is hard to find. Worse than that,
he is eternally reproducing himself; he
brings forth a brood, or rather like the worm,
the more you divide him the more alive he
becomes; each piece of him in its turn ma-
turing and producing.

He turns your mind into a nest, and wallows in it as the swine wallow in the sty. He loves luxury and splendor as does the harlot; and his beauty, when it glitters has all the fascination of a lewd woman.

The true sage controls his imagination somewhat as he does his memory, putting it out as he would extinguish a lamp, or lighting it as he would kindle a fire. The true sage can build himself an air castle that floats in a cloud, and frescoe it with the pictures of angels. He can conjure forms of grandeur that outrival nature's own work; and create storms, the thunders of which will drown the voice of Jupiter. He can tint the rose and perfume the lily; still further, he can create the NEW, and build palaces that no architect before him has conceived, and design landscapes that as yet, are strangers to the brush. The sage but *wills* and his servant, the imagination, *does*.

On the contrary, he who is unwise, is the coward lackey of his Master Imagination. He grovels at his feet, and hides his head, and stops his ears against the horrors thrust

upon him. He fears the dark, and dreads
being alone. He is tortured about his health,
and magnifies every twinge of pain into the
death agony. All symptoms are to him as
fatal; he sleeps in his own coffin every night,
and is resurrected from the grave every
morning. His dreams are all warnings and
prognosticate some future weal or woe.

His animal instincts run riot, while *he* is
fettered and bound; his progeny haunt him
like bad children, and lean on him for sup-
port. The air is peopled with his loathe-
some offspring, and they follow him where-
ever he goes.

This fate is inevitable to him who allows
his imagination to go rampant. In time,
his will falls to sleep and he becomes like
one in fever—the prey to uncanny dreams—
or like the brandy-soaked victim who is ever
terrified at the reptiles which his diseased
fancy brings forth.

Take your imagination in hand, and hold
it as you would a pair of horses; do not
let it break, but pull on the bit even
though it foams and writhes. To have

your imagination run with you, is to have
it bring you up any where either throwing
you upon the rocks or landing you in the
gutter.

Every one has imagination in some form.
The power to call up images, is in all
normal human minds, and the power to
bid them leave is there also.

The sage can free his mind of either
unpleasant memories or undesired imagination, by an effort of pure will or by a
substitution. It is just as easy to substitute one imagination for another as one
memory for another.

The power to conjure is a ready power
and easy to handle; ghosts, hobgoblins,
saints and sinners will come at a wave of
the magic wand, and if you did but know
it, at another wave they will disappear.

Evil imagination leads to *suspicion,*
this (as a rule) is a *bad tenant.* To be
forever suspecting, is to go through life as
some people go through a kitchen, sniffing
right and left for bad smells; searching
out hidden corners with an eye for finding

fault; weighing all commodities with a pair of test scales, under pretext of detecting theft; or like one who steals into places at unsuspected times on the lookout for scandal; listening at key-holes, prowling like a cat at night, peeping into windows, over-hauling coat-pockets, rummaging desk drawers, talking in ambiguous phrases, dealing in hints, implying everything and saying next to nothing.

All this is the fruit of an ungoverned imagination; and in its train come jealousy and envy—a hideous pair—who trample on hearts and reputations, and mark their trail with a stream of blood.

Catch your imagination while you can, and wither it with a glance of your eye; otherwise it will curse you—and in cursing you, will *curse the world.*

THE BOOK OF REVELATION.

It is not the Koran, nor the Bible, nor the Tripitaka. It is not the sky with its glittering pattern of stars, nor objective nature as manifested in the sea, the mountains, the rocks nor the rivers. It is not hidden in the debris of the past, nor written upon the tombs of Egyptian Kings. It is not stamped upon tables of stone, nor will it come in handwriting upon the wall. No savant will search it out for you in some concealed vellum covered thickly with hieroglyphics; nor will some priest of the future reveal it to you, taken down from the mouth of an angel.

To go far to find it will be to waste your time. To wait to have it come to you, will be às fruitless as the waiting for an impossible Judgment Day.

The Book of Revelation exists, neverthe-
less, and its pages can be counted by
hundreds. It is in many volumes, bound
in skins finer than that of the sheep or the
chamois. Its letters are written in the
three fundamental colors intershaded by
many tints; some of them flash fire, and
some are wet with tears. It is fully illust-
rated with pictures in pigment mixed with
blood, and in etchings of black and white.
The scenes are humorous, grotesque, be-
wildering, sad, ecstatic, divine.

"And where is this book," you ask; I
answer, "Look within, read yourself, and
behold the *revelation*."

The skin covers enfolding each volume
inclose a life of your being—*the fine skin
covers*—the tale is your own sorrowful,
happy story which never ends, but has sequel after sequel eternally. The letters pick
out the emotions, in dark or light, in blood
or fire. The blank pages are your dream-
less sleeping hours; and each sentence points
the moral like the finger of fate.

It is the Book of Mystery—the record of

the dead and the living—its initial letters speak beginnings and the closing word of every page its endings. You can read this book from first to last, or backward from last to first. It *reveals, reveals, reveals.* The more you read, the more you learn. No two pages are alike; no two scenes are the same, yet one flowers out of the other as naturally as the rose from the bud.

It is an inspired book; inspired by Mother Nature, by the Priest of Friendship, by the God of Love, by the King of Evil.

It contains prophesies innumerable and warnings without number. Its sallies of wit conceal an element of sadness; its snatches of pathos, a strain of gladness. In the reading, your eyes travel between the lines, and up and down and right and left. The words form into things and the things become alive; even the thoughts march on in file, a long procession holding volume to volume, as an army spans a river and binds land to land.

This book was used at your christening, and will be brought forth at your funeral.

It is given to you for a plaything in your
cradle and will be folded in your hands in
your coffin.   It is your Sacred Book—your
Bible—your Bhagavat—your Ritual.   It
encases your prayers and your psalms.
Alas! it embodies your evil thoughts and
your woes.

Each letter casts a shadow, and the bright-
est throws the blackest.   It is illuminated
with its own light, and the color of the glow
varies with the turning of the pages.   It is
written in hieroglyphics which you alone
can understand—and even you puzzle over
the letters, when naught but the dictionary
of objectivity can help.

Study the world, that you may find its
final interpretation.

PRIDE AND PHILOSOPHY.

It is not strange that pride is the usual vice of all young Philosophers. By young Philosophers I mean those just beginning the pursuit of a *genuine* system. The first result of ardent and earnest investigation is an increase of power, and with power comes pride. A consciousness of strength makes one teem with self-respect, or in other words an emotion which the vulgar call conceit.

To be a few inches higher than your fellow-men on the ladder, enables you to look down upon them, and alas! to despise them. We condemn self-respect, pride, self-love and self-pity, because to respect yourself is, to a great extent, to be satisfied; and to be satisfied in this sense of self-admiration, is to check all further advancement along the line of consciousness.

A respect of self is simply another way

of being **proud** of self, and this entire **sen-**timent should **be** replaced by a something which puts the contemplation of self, in the petting, coddling, comforting **way,** entirely **out of** your thought.

Pursue **a** thing **for its own** sake—beauty —art—health—happiness, and **in the** pur-suit after the *ideal* **self-respect** will be killed. Do **not be** alarmed, **there is no** danger **of** your **going** wrong in this; **the** object **of** your **pursuit** will **save** you **from** degrada-tion. When you are on the chase, **no one** can hurt you by enticements or allurements. You will not stop to lie **or to steal or** to do vulgar acts. You have **no time to call** names or, in any manner, to **lower your** moral standard.

Other people will honor **your** concentra-**tion and** the **results** produced **by it. You have no need** to contemplate **yourself, or pay homage to your** own **soul.**

Pride is an uncomfortable thing to have **about one ;** it pricks like a paper of pins ; it is easily knocked over, and it falls like lead, and in the overturning makes a noise and attracts everybody's attention. A haughty, self-respecting person is ever sensitive lest his pride shall be hurt, and challenges the world with his satisfied gaze; which world, proceeds immediately upon the challenge to knock him down.

It is not in the least strange that the young Philosopher is proud, because an increased sense of power makes one superior, and being strong, he takes delight in manifesting this consciousness. There are two reasons for this; one is that he sees the littleness of his fellow-man as he never did before (this is right), and the other reason is that he is not yet himself sufficiently in love with the object of his pursuit (say truth) to rise above this enervating consciousness of self (this is wrong). We find ourselves only in something *outside,* never in dwelling on self *emotionally.* To dwell on self in this way is to sap your own life. This has nothing to do with self-contemplation *intellectually,* which is desirable. We prohibit emotional self-contemplation only.

Pride is an emotion, a feeling; self-respect explains itself in its name. It is a warming up of self to self, an admiration of self for self, a gloating over, a feeding upon self. This is one of the *greatest* evils.

When the young man came to Christ and informed him in a self-complacent way, that he had kept all the Commandments from his youth up, the Master requested him to sell all that he had and follow him; meaning, that in pursuit of the *Ideal* he should forget his own goodness.

Do not mistake us. Your final object is to find *yourself,* but you never can do it by self-admiration. As you never have seen your own face except in a mirror, you never can behold yourself except *in another*. When you gaze into the eyes of a friend you find a little image of yourself imbedded there. To find the beauty of the *subject,* you must gaze at the *object.*

Pore over self, look into self, analyze self, dissect self; but never shed one tear upon the soil of your own soul; if you do, something rank and poisonous will grow with roots so deep, that it will take your whole *Unit of Force* to pull it out.

The true Philosopher does not carry his pride with him long. Before he enters the narrow path he is stripped naked and his pride falls first. He is allowed nothing heavy about him, and pride is heavy; he has to run, for he is after something which eludes and evades him. His eye must be steadily fixed on the object or it will escape him; and self-respect would be a fatal encumbrance. He becomes so in earnest in viewing himself in the thing that he is after that he forgets himself altogether; this proves that one who would save his life must lose it in the life of another.

The first sorrow that comes to the young Philosopher is the fall of his pride; when it has been broken he becomes a servant; and that to the very ones upon whom he formerly looked down. "He that is first shall be last." He *stoops* to *conquer*, and when he again holds up his head, it is for the purpose of seeing better, rather than that of looking over the hats of people.

The object of this Philosophy is *to gain power;* not that we may come down on others with crushing blows, but that we may give them a lift upward. You might stiffen your back till you walked like a heathen king, but as your strut becomes intensified your line of equipoise might be overlooked and your next position would be that of a fool in the dirt.

Save your energy for the race; you are supposed to be after something and very much in earnest. Other people will see you running and possibly they will start in too, just for the running's sake, and later on they may find an object to chase.

If you have a vestige of pride left, if your self-respect still lingers; if your self-love whimpers and whines, get rid of them *all.* They will block your way where ever you turn; and as long as you harbor these vices you will get no where. Your haughty looks will set others to laughing; and you will freeze yourself. Before you go farther strangle your pride, lest it get too heavy for you and throw you down.

WHO ARE OUR CRANKS?

What are cranks? Who are they? These questions are easily answered. First let me say, that there are all degrees of cranks, from absolute to comparative; that they range from a fool to a knave and from a king down to a peasant. Let me add also, that they are dangerous every one of them, from the highest to the lowest. A crank is an unbalanced person; by this we do not mean insane, but one whose consciousness is clouded; he wears a veil and does not see straight; he is cross eyed and *intrinsically* evil.

A person may be ignorant and not be a crank; he may see but a short distance but his vision will be correct as far as it goes. He will not have a mountain-top sweep, but he can make out a horse or a dog as truly as could Lord Bacon. Ignorance and short-sightedness do not mean crankism.

A crank has crooked **sight** ; no matter what he sees nor how far, everything is out of gear, distorted. To be **seen** properly even a small thing should be consistent with itself and to the one who sees. A crank's vision is out of focus; not only his physical vision, but his mental and psychical vision as well.

The mass of humanity have a vast deal of common sense. Selfishness develops this very early. The great body of mankind adjust themselves to their environment without knowing why. They avoid spectacles and steer clear of oculists. They have a sort of horse understanding which enables them to find a stable and fodder. Selfishness is the cause of this, but it is a proper selfishness and of a different kind from that of the crank.

If the crank is not born an Egoist he very soon becomes one, for it is almost invariably the love of notoriety that leads him into eccentricities. He longs for some sort of fame, any sort. The idea of the *love of truth for itself* has never entered his head. His first ambition is to be looked up to. He begins by becoming odd, and thus attracts notice. There is so much of the fakir about him, that he grows more eccentric as people stare. If he gets a following, he begins to believe in himself and finally concludes that he is inspired; having no balance, but only love of fame, he does more and more absurd things until the world hisses him down.

His disciples become contaminated with his *unholy* magnetism, and become lesser cranks themselves, rushing with their erratic Master to destruction.

There are religious, scientific, artistic, scholastic, dogmatic cranks ; cranks of both sexes; cranks among the rich and the poor. They run after all sorts of absurdities which have no basis of reason. They like concealment and mystery; they hate the light of the sun and sense. Alas ! a vast proportion are women, whose little minds dabble right and left in mysterious cults, that they may have hobbies and fads. They bring greater cranks to their drawing rooms to lecture them on X plus nothing, and that they may drink in *words* as a toper swallows rum. They ask no questions other than, "Is it new?" "Is it strange?" They never once inquire "On what is it based?" "Is it sound?" They *abhor* logic, evidence and facts; they *adore* theories, dreams and asser tions. They love one who will state to them something in positive tones with divine authority. They delight in being hypnotized by fools more foolish than themselves. They glory in the Kingdom of Fooldom and long to dwell there forever.

Talk to them in plain Saxon, and they accuse you of being rough; present them a syllogism and they dub you as dry; preach to them plain facts, and they call you common; give them experience and they banish you at once. They desire and promulgate hypotheses and theories; they stand with each foot on an assertion and shake their fists at reason.

You will find the crank on nearly every

street of **every city** in America, to say nothing of Europe **and** the Holy East. But the
Arch Crank is rarer; and like the **Chief
Devil** is slippery **and evasive.** He is **around**
though, and **he has one** quality **that the**
ordinary crank has not—*wickedness;* his
very crankiness is **abnormal** self-interest
and sin. Beware of the others, but very
much of him ; he is horned **and** hoofed and
clawed. **He** can hurt **you** with his **head** or
his feet or his hands, even with his eyes.
In fact, His Majesty the Prince of Evil, is
a crank, if crookedness means anything.

You ask anxiously, **"How** shall we recog-
nize those who are truly clairvoyant and
honest ? " **By one** simple rule—a *common
sense* seeker after synthetic truth for truth's
sake is never a **crank.** If he is in earnest,
fame and notoriety are side issues. He is so
serious that he forgets to pose; **he is** not sit-
ting for his photograph, **he** is engaged in
living. **Life** is **his** object, **not** position; he
may appear **cranky** at times, and exceed-
ingly absurd, but **his** motive, if he let you
see it, will **clear his** name. The would-be

Sage often seems like a fool, but to *look* the crank and to *be* one, are vastly different.

"Are there no honest cranks?" you ask. Yes, a few. They are the great specialists, who have scarcely any power of *generalization;* they accomplish something in one particular line, but their vision is narrow; they see straight ahead, but they cannot look out at the sides. They have a defect of vision which the doctors find hard to cure.

The all-round Sage has eyes peering to all points of the compass. Try to "evolute" eyes; the more eyes you have, the less of a crank you will be.

ONE DAY.

In the dark we dream of the dawn and youth — divine youth — starry-eyed. We pray for the morning—and the flash—a sky warm with the bud of passion—a form soft-limbed and strong. It comes—We have prayed. It comes—morning—youth.

We stand somewhere on a high place, and thrill with our blood—and the sunrise. The bud steals' up on the sky like the promise of a fiery rose—the blood mounts to our cheeks like a prophesy of creation. But it is opening—the great flower. The sky quivers with red rapture—youth is fulfilled —passion is rising—our soul is on fire.

Alas! We stare at the sun and he puts out our eyes—the new sun—the young sun —he stabs us with needles of light till pleasure is pain. And our passion—the

flower of our youth—pierces us through and
through till ecstacy weeps.

Alas! **We** long for the *noon* — the
climax—the zenith. We go in the dark
and wait.

Up the **high path** of the sky the sun
triumphantly marches—and we wait in the
dark. The *noon* of our life—the climax—
the zenith—when glitters the mind **like**
steel in the battle—when the heart beats
time to the fight—when our muscles are
hard like a rock—our nerves tense like the
string of a bow.

Alas! We uncover our heads and **go**
out at the stroke of the clock—High noon
when the mass is said and the aged die—
And we stare, but the sun more cruel than
fate pierces us through with its darts. We
are blind—struck by the light.

Alas! Our blood had grown **rich**—**we**
were ripe—our muscles and nerves were
tense—our heart beat time **to the** march of
our feet—We lifted our arm, our strong
right arm, and hurled the lance—It was
noon—it struck at the sun in the zenith

above, and backward it flew to our heart—
straight to our heart. The rose of our
passion was dead—killed by our strong
right arm.

We go in the dark and pray—pray for the
eve and the setting sun—for the splendors
that usher in night, when the stars of hope
come out. We pray for the calm of our
poisoned blood—for the cool of the slow
heart beat—for the quiet of sleep—for
comforting dreams.

Alas! the sun goes down and we stare
in its face—but our eyes are gone—eaten
by worms—the worm of *age*. And we fall
to the ground for our limbs are weak—
they shake with years. And we look within
but we cannot see, for our blood is cold and
thick—our heart is ice, and beats with a
noise like the cracking of snow.

Alas! Alas!! But wait!!! The GODS
do face the *sun*. BE GODS.

SECRET GRIEF.

You will understand it, and how impossible it is to seek sympathy anywhere. You would go to the rack ere you would tell it; torture could never force it from you. You hide it and hide it deeper and deeper for fear some far-reaching eye will pierce to the secret. It is yours, emphatically yours. Your closest friend never suspects it, or if he does he cannot divine it. Shame would paint your face redder than roses if it were dreamed of; not the shame of guilt, but the shame of shyness. You know that no mortal can comprehend it, no mortal but you; even God must be puzzled about it you are sure. It is utterly inexplicable, and simply *is* as life is. It is something so foreign to what you would tolerate in another, that you wonder that you nurse it in yourself.

It is altogether out of the Conventional, and has a close kinship to Mother Nature unpainted and unpowdered by the hand of Civilization.

It is an enigma, and yet you comprehend it in a way and feel that it is the key to yourself. Could you discover the meaning of it, you would know who you are, what you have been, and will be. Your Secret Grief is sacred; it dwells in your innermost heart where no other may enter. It puts your character in a strange light—the after-glow of a long gone past floods it, and the dawn of tomorrow gilds its edge. It is not so much something that you have done, as a something that you have felt and still feel; a something that Society says you shall not feel; that man prohibits. As if Society and man could stop the natural beat of the heart, and escape the brand of Cain.

It may be a secret love which the very secrecy sanctifies. It may be a secret hate, which God suffers. It may be an unfulfilled aspiration at which the world would laugh. It may be a memory upon which

Priests frown and God smiles. It may be a regret which grows like a tropic palm, because of your scalding tears. Whatever it is, it is not as *man* would have it, and you are satisfied. You wander in the wilderness with your Ishmael and no one sees. It is your sacred property, the text of your scripture. It is the unnatural child, dearer to the mother than the one born in wed-lock. It is the wild flower, sweeter in scent than the garden rose. It is the crystal spring, hid in the height of inaccessible mountains. It is the ocean depth which the plumb line misses. It is the star out of sight which pulls on the planets. Stop a moment! Think! Now do you *know?* Do you *understand.*

There are open secrets, honorable sorrows, respectable griefs where mourners stand about, and sympathizers swarm. There is priceless crepe, there are flowers and coffins satin-lined. The minister condoles and prays, and angels stop their ears. There are donated years when sorrows sit down in the house, well dressed in black; when comforters come and go, in black; when light steals into the eyes through black—respectable black—and the clock calculates the time for the wearing of black—and the seasons are ravens in black.

But one with the Secret Grief steals up to his room alone and looks out in the dark on the sky, and catching a glimpse of the moon he melts her with his eyes. The moon of flint floats in the mist—the *mist of his eyes*. He locks the door and bids his Secret Grief come forth. Her face chiseled by Destiny defiantly meets his own. She kisses him. Her form, hewn by the Fates, enfolds him. Her hair, shaded from dark to light by the ages, entangles him. Her Karmic eyes meet his and absorb them. Her teeth, hardened by time, bite with their passion his tender flesh. He writhes and quivers in throes of delicious despair. He loves her, and the more he loves the more she tortures. She melts into him and is lost again—deep—deep in his heart.

Then, calmly and unflinchingly he carries her about in the mart of trade, to church

even to his own fire-side. He talks with
friends; they know not. He smiles in
women's eyes and they smile back. He
dances, eats and laughs. He earns gold and
spends. He studies and invents. He dies.
And when they try to bury him, something
weighs the coffin down—the bearers stagger.
The Grief is there—'tis like a stone. *He
left it when he died.*

COLD DESPAIR.

A feeling of despair once felt, is ever afterward appearing in memory, somewhat as a death escaped comes back torturing like a phantom fiend. Very few on earth have drank the cup to the dregs. To drain the cup, is reserved for the elect.

Sorrow has touched you, and you call it despair. Agony has passed before you, and you name it despair. Pain has vanquished you, and you have imagined despair; but the horrid thing, the never-forgotten thing, comes *rarely*. As long as Hope casts a single ray, despair is not, for the creature glows with its own light—the lurid, sulphuric, blue glitter of hell.

Hope shrouds one in white mist through which the eyes cannot penetrate. Where Hope is, all is white mist—the fog of

illusion.   But despair crawls on its belly,
and lights up the night with the shine
of its scales—phosphorescent like fire-flies.
There are things that are light and cold.
Despair is light and cold—colder than ice—
colder than space—colder than the dead.
To feel its touch, checks the flow of your
blood, and neither the fire nor the sun can
warm you.   You shrink back and back into
yourself, farther, farther back in search of heat
—of the white heat of life.   But the furnace
is cold, the fire smoulders.   Despair waits
his chance.   He bides his time.   He catches
Hope napping, and he freezes her ; and *then,*
he seizes you with his eyes.   If Hope is not
frozen stiff, if she be not stark and dead, she
will arouse and veil your face and Despair
will wander off ; but Memory, like his slimy
trail, will stay.

What can you do, what will you do if he
appear ?

"Fore warned, fore armed."

Despair and Hope are twins, born from
the same womb at the same hour.   The
secret sympathy between the two, you can

not fail to feel. Where one is, there the
other dwells. Though Hope shrouds you
in her veil until Despair is not, beware! for
this illusion veil—this maze of tint and
light—this many colored rainbow shroud—
this cloud of bubbles and dew—this irides-
cent lace entwined with opals, amethysts
and pearls—this dainty dream of splendor
dazzling while it soothes, is but the burial
shroud of truth. It is the mist upon the
microscopic lens. It is the mote within the
telescopic eye. It is the mask upon a
woman's face. It is the fool's cap on the
Sage's head.

In flying from Despair you leave fair
Hope behind. Fair Hope! The aphrodite
of your dreams—the golden-haired—the
amber-eyed. Fair Hope! who points to
something yet unseen—who smiles on something yet unknown.

Truth will have none of her, for like a
harlot, she conceals within her ample skirts
her brother—Cold Despair. She hides him
mid the draperies and dances madly in the
sun—her partner hugged close to her

breast—but when she tires and falls upon
the ground asleep, sometimes alas! sometimes the dew trailed mystery of her robe is
rent, and from her very vitals does her
awful mate come forth. Sometimes—but
you who never dance with Hope, see him
not. Sorrow, agony and pain have been
your guests, but Cold Despair is yet to come.

Beware! beware of *Hope,* and seek ye
wisdom. Truth neither hopes nor fears;
she understands. What she sees is *essence,*
more glittering than illusion in the glare of
fire, more brilliant than all the suns above,
more real than Karma, more enduring than
the Fates. And on the door-post of her
temple there is writ in blood, "He who
enters here, leaves Hope behind."

BEAUTY—ART—POWER.

What is it you desire, Beauty? What for? Is it to please a friend? Is it to win a heart! Is it to gain admiration, flattery or fame, or is it for the love of it?

The object of this Philosophy is *power*. You ask for Beauty for the reason, perhaps, that you love it, but still more for the sake of power. Now pay close attention. The sense of Beauty is in some sense the most pleasing of all the abstractions; for it is a sense and an abstraction. Beauty is that certain combination of things that appeals to us in a manner to fascinate. In this sense it is rather different from all other abstractions. The abstraction lies in the law of the combination. The same things thrown together in some other way, would be governed by another abstraction which would not be that of Beauty.

Suppose you desire this result, Beauty, in

order to please a friend, or to win a heart.
What comes? Beauty, but not in the form
which appeals to the heart you desire to
engage. *It comes to you as you ap-
preciate,* and fails to do the work
desired. You are duped, and have
missed your end. The love of *Beauty*
not being the ultimate, but the love of the
friend, you have neither a reward from the
abstraction nor the desired heart. Alas!
desolation. Your premise was wrong. To
gain power from Beauty you must seek it
for its own sake, leaving out of your mind
all thought of what it will do with
others, and filling yourself with the
idea of what it will do with you. Out of
this goes and comes *Power*. Beauty blesses
you, and with the touch of the tips of her
fingers, you feel the magnetic thrill. Your
magic then over others comes not from your
conception of Beauty, nor your passion for
her, but from the added power which your
consciousness of her bestows.

Your effect upon others comes always
from a concealed power; and a love of Beauty

for itself, aids that power. Having such a
devotion to the abstraction, you find it mani-
fests in form everywhere and always con-
gruous. Beauty is never incongruous ; she
combines well and appropriately. She does
not adorn her sea-nymphs in muslin ball
dresses, nor her belles of the dance in a bath-
ing suit. She puts the right thing in the
right place, and makes it fit to the landscape
and environment.

A woman devoted to the beautiful would
endeavor to be so even on a desert where no
eye, not even her own, could behold her.
She would seek—all things being equal—
for the adored one, and would beg her com-
pany. She would instinctively adorn herself for the Beauty's sake, even though
her conception of her be different from
all others ; and in this converse with the
divine abstraction—harmony manifested in
the *Real*—she would grow strong.

In the world no one can laugh down the
Beauty lover. He is supremely happy in
his divine association and smiles back on
the scorner in his consciousness of power.

Do you desire Art ? What for—for whom ? If for another, to gain by it, to hold another, your quest is vain; but if your motto is, "Art for Art's sake," pray on. Like Beauty, Art is an abstraction growing out of combination. It has a meaning, subtle, and its own. It includes *consistency* and congruity. But Beauty is not necessarily its divine consort.

Art brings holy satisfaction, in fact a species of ecstacy; but the rapture is different from that of Beauty or Love. There is a sense of the dual nature of Truth about Art, which is not found in the glamour of Cupid. In the trail of Art is a stream of blood—on the brow of Art is the shadow of hate—in the eyes of Art is the lust of life.

Art like a white star, twinkles in all tints—fire which burns heaven's blue and blackness. Art is master of heaven and hell—he soars to the zenith and dives to the center. He is awful—he is sweet—he appeals to the worst and the best in you. He is a God, all-sided. He fires you with the lust of a fiend, and inspires you with

the love of an angel. He tempts you to
the low, and beckons you to the high.
Splendid! magnificent! he stands on the
rock-granite foundation of earth, and
lizards crawl over his feet. But the tower-
ing head rears itself into the cold spaces
where feeling is lost in intellect and fear
in knowledge. The heat of the planet's
internal fires warm him—the cold of the
sky's chilling ethers freeze him—Art the
terrible—Art the *divine*.

Would you know him, touch him—kneel
at his feet? Let me whisper a secret—only
for his own sake, will he have you—*only
for his own sake*—And more, while you
crawl near his skirts and pick flowers, he
is likely to tread on your form. He will
think you a worm. Rise up. Stand near,
and measure stature with him. Though
he towers to the stars, stand near. *Dare
thou to stand;* and gazing on him thou
wilt grow taller—taller—elbow to elbow—
shoulder to shoulder—taller—taller—neck
to neck—head to head—eyes to eyes.

Power—Beauty—Art—Power!

SPIRITS AND DEVILS.

We have a good deal to say on this subject, and what we do not put into words
may be easily read *between* the lines.   In
the first place, to go spirit hunting is *bad*
business, unless—here we make a dash—,
for there are conditions.

If you have the scientific mind, which is
nothing other than one bent on knowing
for the knowing's sake; if you are sure of
yourself, you may search after ghosts.
Anything you can find in the Universe is
a good thing, if it comes to you in the form
of a *hard fact.* Do not congratulate
yourself; it is possible that you have not
as yet evolved the scientific mind.

But wait a moment, there is another
condition; perhaps you have lost a friend
—one very much loved; that the living

without him is a long agony; possibly you
have not gone far enough in philosophy to
understand the full meaning of this, so
you call him to come to you—out of the
darkness—out of the unseen—if only
the *vapor* him—that you may know his
breath on your cheek—cold like the wind
of winter, but *his*. Have you the right to
this—you have.

The " touch of the vanished hand " will
set you singing again; only—know this,
that where you head, *there is danger*. In
the wet where the lilies grow, the devil is
hid; those pale ghost lilies spring from the
slime where the wallowing snake lies low.

In the seance room, His Majesty sits,
where the horse-shoe circle divides. He
pays no money and laughs in his scarlet
sleeve when you pay yours. Respectable
ghosts stay away, all SPIRITS except
himself—all. If as savant you seek for a
ghost, keep clear of the seance room
where a fee is paid. And more, look out
for the unseen guest who laughs in his
scarlet sleeve. If you seek for the loved

and lost, keep clear of the seance room
for they *never* come that way.

His Majesty cheats you again in the
guise and form of a bride or a friend.
Some day we will tell you how. Satan
goes round disguised as a ghost, and devils
both great and small emerge from the cur-
tained box—*unseen* but *real*.

DEATH—WHAT OF IT?

———

"If I should die," you say, "If I should die just at the moment when I have learned to live, what good? Philosophy is for life, *life*—but *death!* What has the frozen corpse, embalmed, shrouded, boxed, to do with truth? The charnel-house is a dreary place; the grave is foul; even the mausoleum, touched up with gold, is a lonesome spot. "If I should die—what then?"

Philosophy is for life, we still reiterate, *for life;* nor do we deny that death is stalking up and down the world to meet even you —*you*. Some day the wind will blow— colder than ever before—it will lay you low, and transform you into a fallen statue. The breath of Death! more chill than the winds of the Arctic—Death! He has a twin

brother—sleep—a zephyr of him, yet bleak.
He lowers your pulse and lays you down and
closes your eyes.

Where does Truth sit while you sleep?
Have you watched the sea when the tide is
low—have you heard it sigh in its dreams?

You sleep, and the tide of your life goes
down—down to the ebb—and you sigh in
your dreams; but Truth never closes her
eyes; she watches through night and day
—and she smiles when you sigh—when the
sea sighs.

When you die you will grow so cold that
you will forget to breathe—your brain will
be frozen hard—your lungs will turn to ice
—you will even forget to think—to love.
But wait! Philosophy, garbed in the robes
of Truth will watch the tomb for three long
days, till the butterfly breaks the cocoon;
till the seed bursts open its husk; till the
chick is hatched from the egg; *till the tide
begins to rise;* till the stone is rolled away
and the *Christ comes forth.*

Remember that death is the soil of life

and life is the **despair of death.** Remember
you enter the **womb** to come out; you come
out to return again. What manner of man
goeth in, cometh out; **what manner of man
cometh** out, Philosophy knows. **She meets
her** own at the gate of birth, **and walks by**
his side to the gate of death. **Three days**
in the tomb—three days.

When **you wake** from sleep, **you** take up
the thread and **weave** it into the warp where
it dropped the night before; if **you find it**
knotted—Alas! you left it so. When you
wake from the **ebb-tide** of death and **open**
your eyes in the realms **of** self, you pick **up**
your thread and **weave** again where you
ceased to **weave the** night before. If knotted
—Alas! you left it so.

O loved ones do you **not** see that the silken
cord never breaks ; you pick it up, **now** here,
now there, and you spin, and spin, and spin,
like the sisters of fate. **You** spin as the
spider spins, and **fasten** yourself **to** the web.
You spin with the *silver cord,* **as** fine as a
silken hair, as strong **as** the fiber of life.

The fabric you weave hangs high twixt this
and the other world. 'Tis a veil of gossa-
mer stuff, perfect on either side. You look
through its meshes without—you look
through its meshes within—now standing
in front in the cold—now standing behind
in the heat. 'Tis an endless veil—and you
spin, and spin, and spin—but what do you
spin?

The genius seeks his muse and kneels at
her feet—" O muse! One look from thee—
that I may know eternity."

You who die, remember *Philosophy*—
your muse! She closes your eyelids in sleep,
and sits at your side the long night through.
Dawn comes in, you open your eyes, your
questioning looks melt into hers. She has
watched through the night with steady gaze.
She saw the stars come up and the moon
dip into the sea. Her glance swept the
spaces and comprehended the drama of
earth. She saw Love's rhapsody and Hate's
gore. She beheld sorrow, weeping and pain
writhing. She watched the Mother in the
pangs of child-birth and the sufferer on his

bed of death. All this time you breathed softly—your pulse was low—*you slept.*

When death touches you and the wind blows cold, your muse *stands firm.* She wraps you in her cloak and lays you out. She braces herself against death as a single will defies the universe. She faces the Arctic winds. She sets her teeth, and for three days challenges hell. Out upon her leap the devils of Inferno. She stands fast. Calmly you sleep on—as calmly as the plant sleeps under the snow.

Your muse calls heaven to help her—the saints—the cherubs—the seraphs—the angels—the arch-angels—*God.* She dares with her eyes the terrible glitter of the dog star. She shifts her gaze to the awful flash of Arcturus. She appeals to the majesty of Orion. She draws on the fires of the Pleiades. She summons the combined forces of Hercules. She faces all heaven. Her soul drinks at the firmament—and *you sleep on.*

When the Sage of Athens drank the hemlock his muse shuddered, but stood firm.

When the heart of Christ broke, his muse wept, but lived on. When death meets you, your muse will conquer hell, and face the eternal fires. *Fear **not**.*

NATURE'S JEST.

Our whimsical old Mother Nature is apparently a great jester. So it would seem from the expression of her face, but beware! She may be more in earnest than you imagine.

Madame Beauty stands before her mirror and weeps bitter tears as she drapes herself in rags, but Poverty, off in the corner, laughs and laughs. It is a pitiful picture, but not to Poverty, who laughs and laughs. Beauty might pose for Venus naked—but now! Ha! Ha! How Poverty laughs! There stands the idol of men in the sunlight, with hair that wreathes her round and round—magic hair! so electric that a glint of fire is in it—perfumed hair! Nature's own aroma!

But where is the jeweled barb with which

to fasten it? Beauty is too poor! and her
eyes! Tears make them brighter as dew
freshens the roses! Her white breast is but
half covered—Alas! the rags are rent where
the skin is softest, where the cold strikes
coldest.

Poor Beauty! She is honest—no daub
of rouge, nor puff of powder, nor roue's kiss
has touched her, only the wind nipping at
her ears, and her shoulders and her pink
finger-tips. Her tears freeze in her dimples,
she has forgotten to smile, but Poverty
laughs—laughs till the wind is lost in her
voice—laughs till the sound of the church
bell is drowned—laughs till the city's roar
is faint—and Beauty stares in her bit of
glass, which is lit with the flash of her eyes.

Is Nature playing a joke, or is she adjusting the scales?

Madame Ugliness sparkles with gems.
They shine in her ears—gross ears that
gather scandals and lies, as the pitcher plant
gobbles the flies—they shine round her neck,
gaunt like the arm of a sycamore tree—
wrinkled and old—they shine in her hair

where it clings to her head, as moss in patches sticks to a stone. They shine on her fingers, knotted like claws and destined to scratch—scratch. She is swathed in satin and silk as a mummy is swathed; bound and banded and draped till her cracking bones, and her shrunken flesh and her bosomless chest are rigid and stiff.

She fears to gaze in the glittering lake, she dreads the mirror and shining pool, she shuns reflecting eyes. Wealth stands by and sneers—wealth, her consort, secretly sneers and jingles his money-bags. She is so ugly he covers her up with things of beauty, and sneers; he piles on more and more and sneers and sneers.

But what of Nature—the Wise? Does she jest when she brings forth Beauty and sends her adrift with rags on her back, while hugging Ugliness close to her breast where the rich milk flows?

Ah! Beauty! thy rags but *emphasize thee*—the white of thine arms, the pose of thy limbs. Thine hair is thy robe. The sun is thy love. Thou holdest thy glass.

But Ugliness—thou? Can **Nature balance the** scale where beauty is weighed? She loads on the silks, the satins, the furs; she heaps on the rubies and gold, she piles in the diamonds, the **emeralds, the pearls,** and yet, even yet, Beauty is heavy, gold is a feather, the jewels a speck. And Nature, de-spairing, goes down to the sea, she dives for more jewels, and more, she digs into earth and brings up more treasure and more. She slaughters the beast and the bird, she tears off the hide and the plume, but Ugliness crouches, light as the skin of a fish, while Beauty outbalances all.

Ah! Nature! you jest, unless time and causes long gone can be caught to weigh down things as they seem.

YOUR FRIEND.

Is he hateful today—think of tomorrow, remember last week. Is he scowling, recall his smile. Has his tongue twisted itself into harsh words—forget not the sweet ones you have caught from his lips.

Do your friend justice. Place him on the scale of your own conjuring and weigh yourself with him. Perhaps after all he is heavier, a better man than you. When you judge another make two columns in your mind, the pros and cons. Reckon them up as you would a sum, and subtract one result from the other. If there is more good than bad—more that is delightful than repellant—more sweetness than gall, hold fast to him forever. You have found a jewel, one with a flaw to be sure, but a jewel. It is not

paste nor pebble, but a gem. It will
flash in a comparatively dark place, brighter
than in the sunshine. Wear it on your
breast, and look into the glass when the
light is dim. But if the balance is against
him, if the cons outweigh the pros, avoid
him. He may shine for another, but not
for you. By no amount of polishing can
you make a diamond of him, or a ruby, or a
pearl. Another may, but not you.

Never let your heart deluge your head,
when friendship comes your way. The head
must be above tears and smiles—in clear
cold air—where it can think.

The heart is a fountain whose stream
flows forever, warm and gushing. You can
not stop it nor would you. But keep your
head high, that you may see clearly, to turn
the course of the waters where the flowers of
friendship can best grow. It is better to
overlook a field of ice with cold judging
eyes, than to raise a crop of weeds in a soil
watered by tears.

Be just to your friend and you will deal
squarely with yourself. Await his coming

—It may be a long time ere he appears—
You can afford it—wait.

Jewels are not used for side-walks, nor
stars for street-paving. You may find the
pearl in the oyster you would eat, possibly
at the retailers. Be sure it is a pearl before
you set it. If it is precious conceal it, for
there are thieves about. If it is luminous
hide it, for it might dazzle some one else.

Your friend is your own—not anothers—
in *that* which makes him yours; otherwise
go friendless, and live with the birds, the
mountains and the sky. In nature some
aspect of *you* is concealed, find that.

THE ONE THING.

Man wearies of everything save *one*. He plucks the flower he has striven after, inhales its perfume and withers with it. Every thing tires him, even the most loved. When the flame goes out, he finds ashes—black and gray. No outer splendor holds his eye long. He turns wearily from the vale to the mountain, and again from the mountain to a star. In the face of the star he closes his eyes. *He is tired,* even of the smile of his loved friend. At times he would fly from it. He wearies of the days of his youth—He throws no kiss after them —He is glad they have gone—He wearies of his prime and seeks to escape it, into the easy chair of age. He wearies of old age, and of the old clothes which alone suit it. He makes his own coffin while yet alive. He drives the nails himself, and longs to lie down therein, even before he dies. He is tired—surfeited with everything.

This is the **natural man, the man of**
rhythm.　He **rubs off the down from the**
peach and eats **it—He wins a heart to**
trample it—All because he **is tired.** Because the demon—change—has told **but**
half his story, shutting its mouth **in the**
midst of the tale.

　But **the One** Thing—What of the **One**
Thing? Is there somewhere a **bird of para-**
dise whose feet never **touch the earth? Is**
there a gem that **charms the eye** to flash
ever? Is there a flower that excites one to
ecstasy by its breath? **Is** there a song that
one sings always? Is there a land where
the grass never withers? Alas! no. The
One Thing is subtle and mighty—It dwells
out of sight. No eye has beheld it nor **ear**
heard its voice. Philosophy—Truth—fas-
cinating as the Ideal, faithful as the Real,
ready at all times every where to fit change
to change—as the lapidary fits gem to gem
—linking incident to incident, mood to
mood, hour to hour, day to day, year to year
with the goldsmith's art. Of IT—This
power which ties and binds, holds and con-

nects, fits and matches—you never weary.
The mood may worry you, the day may ex-
haust you, but the art to adapt and link
them, is the Master Creative Art—the
magic power, which if once you feel, will
reveal the ONE THING.

The charm of conquering, solving, blend-
ing, combining, is the charm of God. It is
the power which adapted Earth to the Sun
and Venus to Mars. It is the potency
which patterns the constellations and
spangles the sky with starry designs. This
master power of adjusting our moods and
our hours one to another—this art of sway-
ing to environment, has in its essence the
charm of the new—The ecstasy of creation
—This *Art* is the Philosopher's own. The
normal man knows nothing of it—He is
forever tired—but the Sage smiles at pros-
perity, and goes with it, as man does with
woman even to the precipice of adversity,
where he smiles again and ties a knot—He
has bound the two firmly like husband and
wife, and he blesses them both. The Philosopher bares his head to the gale and lets

the wind's sharp fingers tear at his blowing hair—He suffers the knives of ice to prick to his bones—He tests himself on the grindstone of fate—and finds the *new*.

Each morn a new sun peers over the borders of dawn—Each eve a new splendor melts into the bosom of the night—Each day is a virgin immaculate, who conceives and gives birth to a Christ. A mystery appalling, but sweet, challenges the Wise with each fresh beat of his heart, for to him is given the *One Thing*—the *power to Create*.

All other men tire. They sicken with the stench of the *old,* the fetid, the stale. They shrink from the same dull colors and shapes—the picture comes back at each turn of the wheel—*the same*. They start at familiar sounds, the shriek of the whistle, the roll of the drum—the same from cradle to grave—the same—But the Sage! He touches the old—A Philosopher's touch—as soft as the falling of snow—the kiss of a friend—and lo! the *new*.

THE DEVIL.

He **is out of** fashion. He went off the stage with Jonathan Edwards and men of his cult. **The** masters of the " new theology " have not fist enough to shake at his phantom, so they deny him. They stand in their pulpits and preach goodness, love, music, flowers, paradise. They believe in **an** eternal heaven of splendors without the " great white throne." They have banished the angels and the harps, and they **give** you Nature (when she smiles). **The storms** they ignore. When the wind blows **they become** as deaf as stones—They hear **nothing.** When it is cold, they sit over **their church** furnaces and declare it is **warm.** They are

as one-sided as the moon. If they have
another face, they conceal it. This is
" namby-pamby." It is gush.

We face facts. We believe that everything has two sides. If there is an up,
there is a down. If there is a white, there
is a black. We know very well that lilies
thrive in mud, and roses in decay. We have
seen the cat eat the mouse and the dog kill
the cat. Insects destroy trees, and elephants
tread on worms. We are also aware that
man builds his ladder to fame out of dead
bodies, and climbs to the stars to the tune
of dying shrieks. The sea fish gorge themselves with one another, the air fiends in the
shape of birds dive out of heaven after
helpless victims.

You may call the Devil by whatever name
you choose, *evil is a fact* or good could not
be. We believe in the *Pairs*—the *Paral-
lels*. Life and death go arm in arm. Pain
and pleasure are close linked. Heaven is
on the verge of hell. God implies the
Devil. We believe he takes a thousand
forms, a *million*, a *billion*. He is not con-

fined to hoofs and claws. Like that of Good
his coat is "many-colored."

We have told you to practice. We have
spoken emphatically, and you ask with
reason—"On what?" On the Devil. He
is the best muscle developer known. He
can put you through a regular course. He
will teach you to aim a straight blow and
hit between the eyes. To be sure you will
be knocked down over and over again, but
get up. To lie and groan is to give him a
chance. You must be quick, as quick as he
is. You will grow as strong as a Greek
athlete, and be ready for the ring on all
occasions. He does you a good turn in giv-
ing you the chance. In time you will glory
in ycur own strength as a young man does.
In fact the Devil is mightily afraid of the
Philosopher, he prefers the nervous man,
one who loses his head.

Philosophy is the "*bete noire*" of the
Arch Fiend. He fears naught else than
that. There is a smile on the Sage's lip
that makes his majesty shrivel. There is a
steadiness in the wise man's eye that galls

even the Devil. He is sarcastic, but the Philosopher is more so—and when the fire fights fire, you know the outcome.

So then we accept him, as we do the other side of heaven, for the inner implies the outer—The height the depth.

THE PAIRS.

One's illusions vanish one after another ;
what today we deem real tomorrow will be a
dream. We are building day after day upon
the shifting sand, and the tide comes up and
washes the shining bits away. Hopes
fondly cherished break like bubbles or drown
our hearts in tears.

By and by our eyes will be dry, no tears
will come, and we will stare dimly and
straight ahead into vacancy, to see nothing,
not even an illusion. Then upon all men
we will smile a ghastly smile, hoping for,
believing in, wanting *nothing.* At this
point we reverse and look in. Something
appears, some one, and that appearance, that
one makes the illusion plain. This appear-

ance which looks into our eyes is the *Real,*
the everlasting mate of the *Unreal.*

Had you not dreamed—Had you not suf-
fered—Had you not sobbed on your pillow
at night alone—alone—Had you not longed
and longed when the stars came out—Had
you not begged the grass-blades to speak to
you, and the leaves to whisper to you—Had
you not looked on the back of your friend
whose eyes were turned elsewhere—Had the
sky not rained on you, and the sea sought
to clutch you—Had the mirage not come
nor the dim island faded, the *Real* would
have failed.

Mortal man goes on and on, plodding and
plodding; he eats, he drinks, he sleeps,
alas! he does not dream. His wife makes
his bed and his bread. The beasts in his
yard are his kin. *He dies.* No castle ever
faded out of his sky. No bird with fire-tinted
wing flew over his head; and the *Real*—
the *face* he has failed to see.

When you have drank the wine down to
the dregs—When the golden bowl breaks—
When love flies off to the moon—When

the blood congeals and will not flow, and
Beauty flaunts her hair in your face, *look in.*

The bank must need follow the fickle
river, the inconstant river, but on the bank
the water-rushes grow. Ah! the meander-
ing stream. Ah! the constant shore and
the water-rushes. When drowning in the
cruel river, forget not the shore and the
faithful reeds. Wet and dripping you seek
refuge deep within the rushes—*deep* within
the rushes.

Drenched in the fog of illusion you rush
inland and look into a pair of *faithful*
eyes. I have brushed the cob-webs from
mine forever, the spider's web, and now I see
straight to the heart of a star. But to my
friend I am a mystery. Now and again he
hates me, and yet he loves me too. He
turns here and there for something better ;
he tries to go; he lies to himself, *but he
comes back.*

Look well to the opposites. The Pairs
are faithful. The dream, the illusion, is the
other half of the Real. It shimmers like
the light on the sea—It goes and comes like

the moon—It lives and dies like ripe corn, but the arc of heaven which Iris bears in her hands, overshadows her *never*. Iris still brings news from heaven and tells the tale of Zeus.

ADONAI.

To invoke Adonai is to call upon that in
your universe of consciousness which is
akin to the ecstasy of love, by no means a
physical, but a purely spiritual emotion.
You call out of yourself, into your consciousness, the charm and holy glamour of being.
You throw yourself, by an effort of will, into
a state where soul is manifested in its
beauty, as the flowers display the sex-charm
of plants.   You call up from the depths of
soul its melody, for soul in its most gracious
form is music, the singing as it were of the
bird to its mate.

To invoke Adonai is to enter the world of
variety where habit is abandoned, drudgery
forgotten, and conventionality is no more.
All things *common* are hid from view.   It
is the world of form, of sound, of languor,
and of dream.   It is the world of haze and

splendor — the illumined — the shadowy. Here time ceases, the past melts away, the future is unforeshadowed.

You ask, "Is Adonai a spirit, a Being?" We answer, there is a Being, there are Beings who revel in this Paradise, who hear these sounds and see these sights —Beings who dwell forever in a dim glory softened by a veil such as fell over Isis— Beings whose sight is clouded by tears of rapture, more entranced than those who smile—Beings who hear voices echoing back and forth along the spaces of Heaven— Beings who see tender colors when their eyes are closed, and one of them the Mystics call Adonai.

Life that throes and throes till each throb sings—Life born out of continence till every nerve is thrilling with its own identity, is the spell which Adonai weaves upon himself till he twines his form in rainbows and flashes light from his deep eyes, even as the sun throws flame.

Adonis kissed too much by Venus drags his wings—Adonis free soars upward.

" Can we " you ask, " Can we as Mystics invoke Adonai? " We answer, unless you do, you are doomed to see, to face and struggle with the *common place.* Crude ugliness will strike you hour after hour hard blows—The soul of things will be hid, and only the half of every story will be told—Your nostrils will be greeted by bad smells—Your eyes with ugly sights —Your ears will hear revolting sounds— The barren wash-day grayness of the world will stare you in the face—Your friends will unveil all their petty faults, the very pimples on their foreheads will stand out— The great beyond in them will be boxed up in illshaped skulls—Their tongues will say rough things and lap coarse food—*Ordinary,* all ordinary.

You have no power to discern what they have brought to you, what they yet will bring—You measure but the size of their shoes, and count the spots ou their clothes—You have no gift for looking back nor seeing far ahead—You are marching in the ranks where grease and oil besmirch the

hands of artisans—You smell of lumber, of
fresh fish and blood—You toil till sweat
soaks through your clothes, and gazing up
you think it rains.

Your mother is a woman who breeds and
nurses young—Your father is a man who
gloats and drinks—Your brothers kill live
things, and laugh—Your sisters stuff rag
dolls—Your wife courts your stomach—
And gnats and insects suck your blood.
You have no heaven nor hell. *You serve
the common place.*

But lo! how this doth change when you
besiege the pearly gates of your own heart,
and to the *half truth* add the *other half.*
Does he come in the sunlight of morning or
the sunlight of evening—It matters not.
Does he look down from the zenith or up
from the depths—What difference? Does
he appear without or within—Who cares?
He is Adonai the Beautiful! With him
you get the full meaning—the illumination
—the glory. When you see him, your feet
scorn the earth—When you hear him, you
answer back.

Venus adores and yet fears him, for he scatters light as he moves, and the flashes heat and thrill you. His countenance beams even though veiled, and his eyes pierce and transfix you. All things seen through the mist of him are beautiful. Beside each leaf on the tree is another like silver, which the sun turns to gold.

To invoke Adonai is not always to bring him. Oft times he is taken by force like the kingdom of heaven. If he will not come by your wooing, plunge down in yourself and drag him out of the depths, for he may be asleep.

Beware of the common place. Better look into heaven one moment and down into hell the next, than to set your house in strict order, starch up your linen, and eat for the palate.

Beware of the common place—That mood where you yawn and stretch, and hunt out your aches and pains as old people do, who gloat over sores and decay. Beware of scavengers, buzzards and flies.

MAGIC.

You may follow Christianity to the yawning grave, you may suck the breast of Buddhism dry, and yet miss Magic—an Aphrodite poising on the foam of the sea.

The magician can subtract glamour from the heart of things ; he can manipulate combinations—he can balance on foam. Out of himself comes a magnetism which envelops and transforms environment. As love turns hell into heaven, so the magician plays at his art.

Nature covers the woman's skeleton with voluptuous curves of flesh—She spreads a pond of slime with water-lilies—She bids exquisite ferns to peep from ghastly crevices —She paints the sky at the brink of the desert—*sometimes*—when the mood is on her—*sometimes.* She touches up the vulture in the empyrean, till he has the majesty of a heaven sent messenger—She glitters in the purity of the gull till he rivals a white-throated angel—On winter she breathes, and brings hot splendor out of snow and fire out of ice.

Magic never goes naked—She is as real as the soul of woman, but she drapes herself as did Isis. Her eyes look at you through the veil of her hair—her limbs gleam but from the meshes of a net—She has the art of the spider; she catches and holds, but unlike it she never devours you.

Her food is the pollen of flowers, her drink is the dew on their breasts.

Truth is truth, but she is sometimes noncommital. Whatever she bestows is *one* aspect of her—not all. Veiled in glamour she gives you her smile, and bewitches, tantalizes, lures, and bewilders. Her form is clear-cut and awful, like the scars on the brow of Olympus, but her smile is myriad and seen through a veil.

Mystery and Magic are some way related.

The half known transfixes you—its spell pierces you, like the glance of a wise man's eyes. The mystery of the moon is in Magic —The side which you wonder about is the half that charms. If the satellite turned, Love's dream would vanish.

We hear strange rumors of Adepts in Thibet and the fakirs in India. We have read fairy tales about the miracles of Christ, and the wonder working of Mahomet. We are familiar with the account of the birth of Gautama, and the magic of Moses. In the face of it all we would tell you, that this is as the blowing of a soap bubble compared with the mystery of the seed or the passion of the plant.

Nature is a hypnotist and a magician. She arrests the busy man in his round of work, and holds him spell-bound before a growing grass blade—She stops the devotee of science on his road to fame, and bewitches him with the remains of a mastodon—She glitters in the scalpel of the surgeon, and flashes on the edge of the dissecting knife— She rouges the consumptive's cheek, and tantalizes Esculapius with microbes—She tempts the diver to risk the jaws of the shark, and turns the ills of the oyster into pearls—She foils the explorer with her North Pole, and entices the aeronaut to a pitiful rivalry with the chick-a-dee.

The poet is her victim par excellence. He sees things through the mist of his own eyes—a trait from nature by the terrible law of heredity. He is eternally hypnotized and walks about in a dream. Nature's spell is on him from birth to death, and he, as her true child, shines by his own light. He is not a planet but a lesser sun, that warms itself at its own fire. He generates heat and radiates it from his eyes and fingers. Cold people sit at his feet, as beggars lie out in the light. The rabble follow him as the poor followed Christ. They touch his skirts and warm their bodies in electric heat. Like the magician of India, he draws an ignorant crowd, who know nothing except that he is warm. Each word of his is a spark, which sets something on fire. He is rich with smiles, that tickle the half-dead nerves, and metaphors that shock the heart to renewed life. He moves in a glory like the column of fire, and he casts a shadow like the fallen cloud. He is Ariel captured by Earth. He is a god wedded to woman.

But what of Venus Urania, who makes matches in heaven, and kindles her heart at the shrine of Vesta. What of the love that blends souls rather than bodies, and creates her children in celestial spaces on the down pillows of ether? What of the splendor of Eden, when the gods walked in the garden, and the serpent lay hid in the glitter of his own skin? Even yet magic eyes sweep the horizon, where the sky lies softly on the breast of the sea. Even yet, on the altar of Vesta, burn the sacred fires. Even yet, the loves of paradise hold the sun in its place—and the moon.

Would you know the art of Magic? Would you discover the magician in yourself and wake him out of sleep? Retire within, far back, away from things seen by the natural eye; and the long-lashed lids of a spirit's orbs will unloose—when, lo!

the land of dream! the realm of memories
stored by the ages *in you.* But look—still
farther back, to the magic region of ice and
storm and snow, when the world, like a cold
corpse, lay wrapt in her icy shroud—you,
you were there. Or into those tropic regions
where strange plants grew, watered by mists,
heated by a seething immensity of sun—
you were there.   Or, if your eyes weary
with wonder, and the fringed lids drop,
listen ! Hark with the ears of a spirit
—backward—down the aeons of time. Listen
to the crashing of the avalanches of the
terrible ice period, when chaos roared as the
captain shouts in a storm at sea. Listen to
the strange note of a long-lost bird that
lived in the days of a terrible sun. Listen
to the voice which spoke to you, ere Christ
traveled the banks of the Galilee, or Caesar
mastered the spirit of Rome. *It is speaking still.*

Magic !! Away with the fakir fraud, who
gives you a lie for a paradox—while truth is
truth. Away with the mummery of a false
act and a sham occultism—while the Phil-

osopher's stone exists. Away with the devil's cauldron or the craft of priests— while the great laboratory of nature, manipulated by the witches of science, is seething with the heat of *divine* alchemy.

Would you be a magician, stir up the smoldering coals at your own fireside. Begin to burn. Feel your blood hot in your veins. Warm yourself with memories of sun-tinted dreams. *Pray—pray—pray* at the shrine of the Sphinx.